1951-2006

Donald Freed

BROADWAY PLAY PUBLISHING INC
New York
www.broadwayplaypublishing.com
info@broadwayplaypublishing.com

First printing: December 2011
I S B N: 978-0-88145-508-3

Book design: Marie Donovan
Page make-up: Adobe Indesign
Typeface: Palatino
Printed and bound in the U S A

1951-2006

Donald Freed

BROADWAY PLAY PUBLISHING INC
New York
www.broadwayplaypublishing.com
info@broadwayplaypublishing.com

ABOUT THE AUTHOR

Donald Freed's plays, prizes, books, and films include:

INQUEST (directed by Alan Schneider); SECRET HONOR (directed by Robert Altman); CIRCE AND BRAVO (with Faye Dunaway, directed by Harold Pinter); THE QUARTERED MAN; ALFRED AND VICTORIA (A LIFE); and VETERANS DAY (with Jack Lemmon and Michael Gambon).

Three Rockefeller Awards; two Louis B Mayer Awards; Unicorn Prize; gold Medal Award; Berlin Critics Award; N E A award for "Distinguished Writing"; Hollywood Critics Award; and the Jonathan R Reynolds Prize.

Agony in New Haven; Executive Action (novel and film with Mark Lane); *The Glasshouse Tapes; The Spymaster* (Book of the Month); *In Search of Common Ground* (with Erik Erikson, Kai Erikson, Huey P Newton); *The Existentialism of Alberto Moravia* (with Joan Ross); and *Death in Washington.*

New books, plays and films include: THE EINSTEIN PLAN (with James Cromwell); IS HE STILL DEAD (with Barbara Dana as Nora Joyce); SOKRATES MUST DIE (with Mitchell Ryan); DEVIL'S ADVOCATE (at the Los Angeles Theater Center and York Theatre Royal); and a new novel, *Every Third House.*

Donald Freed is Playwright in Residence at the Los Angeles Theater Center and York Theatre Royal.

CHARACTERS & SETTING

MARGARET ANN MCNALLY, *age: 31 to 86*

DAVID NATHAN LIGHT, *age: 28 to 58*

TOM GUINN, *age: 40 to 89, doubles as* LANDLORD; NEW LANDLORD; F B I AGENT

VICTOR GORDON, *the new tenant, a Puerto Rican dance student; doubles as* WOUNDED REVOLUTIONARY.

Time: 1951 to 2006

Place: A brownstone apartment building on East 87th Street, Yorkville, Manhattan, New York City.

MISE-EN-SCENE

Time: The time span of the play is 1951 to 2006.

The timeline is spelled out on three basic "clocks": 1) The date of each scene is projected onto a wall of the set; 2) certain radio or television news headlines heard from inside the apartment building; 3) the advancing age of the characters, their clothing, behaviour, *and*, in DAVID's case, two or three wheelchairs over the decades.

Sound: A continuous soundscape covering the years from the late 1940s to 2006; the sounds of America and the Building.

Place: The single setting is the top landing of a brownstone apartment house. On this fourth floor landing, there are two apartment doors, 4A and 4B. The audience can see a section of the last flight of stairs that leads up to the fourth floor. There are wall lights on the landing, a skylight, and large wall window, stage right. The characters enter their apartments but the audience never sees more than a slice of the interiors.

Characters: Four actors play all the roles in this story: MARGARET ANN MCNALLY is played by one actor, over a span of 55 years.
DAVID NATHAN LIGHT is played by one actor, over thirty years of this same 55 year period.

TOM GUINN: The third actor portrays this character over a forty-nine year span. This performer also delineates three other male roles: OLD LANDLORD; NEW LANDLORD; F B I AGENT.

ACT ONE

(A Time Capsule of 1940-1950 plays in a loop from Half-Hour until curtain: a radio and early television orchestration of historical figures; popular music; comedy; film.)

(At curtain, houselights low; the legend on the wall reads: "1950: William Faulkner Nobel Prize Acceptance Speech.")

(The great appeal ends. Houselights out. Stage lighting for ACT ONE, Scene 1. Sounds of the building and the street register.)

Scene 1
December 1951, 4 P M

*(Twenty seconds, then a man in a wooden wheelchair—*DAVID NATHAN LIGHT—*bursts out of his apartment, 4A, at speed and wheels to the large window, right, and peers out with an urgent need. He looks and cranes, then wheels sharply up center to the head of the stairs. He leans and listens for something, in vain.)*

*(*DAVID *turns and wheels, down center. His panting now becomes a series of groans and gasps of pain. These involuntary sounds of suffering are interrupted by the distant sound of a street singer in a courtyard below. The man sings the first verse of* Molly Malone.)*

(The song rivets DAVID, *as if it were a signal; as he slowly turns and aims his wheelchair toward the open door of the other apartment on the landing, 4B—dark and empty.)*

*(*DAVID *pushes to the doorway, stops to gather all his strength in order to wheel into the darkness of 4B and, there, to kill himself.)*

(At the last moment, DAVID *hears a cough and footsteps on the stairs. He races his chair to the top of the staircase, strains to hear: ...Yes! The steps are coming up past the third floor to, this, the landing. Now, he shoots into his apartment, 4A, and closes the door just as:)*

*(*MARGARET ANN MCNALLY [MEG] *—31—labors up the fourth flight of stairs, carrying a large suitcase. She reaches the landing, coughs, breathes, tries to center herself. Then, she goes to the window, R, looks out; turns and approaches the empty 4B; hesitates, then turns back toward the stairs as if to leave.)*

(Meanwhile, DAVID *has cracked open his door and has been spying. As* MEG *turns to leave he wheels out singing a Woody Guthrie song. He is wearing dark glasses, now, and a Greek fisherman's cap from the 1930s, and holding a bottle of beer.)*

DAVID: "...If you ain't got the do-re-me-boys..."

*(*MEG *stops, startled, at the stairs to catch her breath.* DAVID *sings to her, then pauses, swigs his beer and stares. He points to her suitcase, she notes his trembling arm and hand.)*

DAVID: ...Need some help?

MEG: Thank-you—no.

DAVID: Warsawski! Hey, *Warsawski!* ...I'll kill him.

*(*MEG *stares back at the open door of the empty room-womb-tomb: 4B.)*

MEG: ...Who's Warsawski?

(DAVID *seizes the moment, wheels center and plays as if to a vast audience.*)

DAVID: Who's Warsawski? Behold the Man! Marshall Abraham Warsawski: The cockroach capitalist in the *bespoke* suit. Ah-Hah—The draft-dodging Fagin, the *goniff*, who just counter-signed your lease. Eighty a month, right? Then he claims he has an emergency across the street at 324, and leaves you to haul your life's savings up four flights, knowing—and this is the point—that I'll have to sit here, helpless, while you, unwillingly, humiliate me—and he's downstairs laughing up his kaftan... Want a bottle of beer? By the way, I'm Jewish, so don't think, ah... You're 4B—

(MEG *tries to interrupt.*)

DAVID: —from Chicago, correct? Irish, Catholic, 31 years old. And by the way, Saint Joseph's on the corner. Go ahead and say a prayer for me— Ha-ha...

MEG: ...Who told you that—about Chicago.

DAVID: Our infamous landlord, our lord of the land— another Chicago boy, "City of the Big Shoulders", as he must have confided to you when he made his first pass. (*Growls*) Warsawski!

MEG: I just have one more small one—downstairs.

DAVID: (*To himself*) Sisyphus.

MEG: "Sisyphus?"

DAVID: Baggage. We all have a "leetle" baggage.

MEG: (*Shaking her head*) Not at all.

(MEG *turns towards the stairs*, DAVID *stops her.*)

DAVID: ...What do you do? My name's David Light, as in "light"...What lies has Warsawski told you about me?

MEG: ...War hero. North Shore family. Twenty-eight years old.

DAVID: Big deal... What about you?

MEG: Margaret McNally. Meg. I teach.

DAVID: I thought so. Nursery school?

MEG: I have... All ages. Some writing.

DAVID: Writing? What?

MEG: ...Anything. Comedy.

DAVID: Comedy? You?

(DAVID *and* MEG *both laugh.*)

DAVID: Me, too.

MEG: You?

(DAVID *and* MEG *laugh.*)

DAVID: No, I'm strictly legit.

MEG: I see. Like what?

DAVID: Oh, the usual: sonnets, haiku, limericks, grand opera. Mainly comedy. I'm a "sit-up" comedian. Didn't you *catch* me—on the Ed *Solomon* Show? "Welcome, Welcome to the Big Show, the Big Show. And here he is, the star of stage and *scream*—Big Dave Luftmensch brought to you by your Armed *Force* Free Radio—direct from Club *Rosenberg* in picturesque Sing Sing New York."

(DAVID *now goes into a Lenny Bruce-like routine, complete with microphone pops and squawks.* MEG *responds with involuntary laughter at the brilliant improvisation.*)

DAVID: "(*Pop-pop-pop*) —Good evening ladies and gentlemen. (*Pop-pop*) Welcome to the back ward of the Long Island General George C Patton Veterans Hospital. (*Pop-pop—screech*) A night to remember: All the *spam* you can eat and a floorshow you'll never

forget: The nurses from the *psycho* ward'll be kicking
up their heels, in their *spanking (He breaks up.)* their
spanking white Eisenhower jackets—costumes and
make up by the Red Cross—and featuring—direct
from twenty-seven weeks in Adolph Hitler's bunker,
direct from Berlin—

(MEG *and* DAVID *are both caught up with laughter.*)

DAVID: Ah-hah! Berlin—in her first American
exposure—Fraulein Fritzy Ritz! Put your hands togezzer
and giff her a real old-fashioned red, vhite, and blue
velcome!"

(DAVID *breaks into a rendition of* Deutchland Uber
Alles. *Before* MEG's *eyes, he is transfigured from Hitler to
an Auschwitz inmate clawing on barbed wire. Pause. He
drops the tortured tableau, takes off his glasses. She has been
stunned, has put down her suitcase and now stares at the
man in the wheelchair.*)

DAVID: ...O K, what's the verdict? ...A thousand bucks
and it's yours.

MEG: *(Pause)* Can I read some of your material?

DAVID: Get out.

MEG: Why? I'm serious.

DAVID: The *unthinking* man's Lenny Bruce, huh?

MEG: ...Forget it then.

DAVID: ...I will!

(MEG *starts to leave, then turns back to look into her new
apartment.* DAVID *stalks her with his chair.*)

DAVID: ...Raskolnikov moved out last week.

(MEG *stares at* DAVID)

DAVID: Want a bottle of brew?

(MEG *turns back to look into the empty apartment, 4B.*
DAVID *creeps up behind her. He uses Irish brogue to cover
his raw sensibilities.*)

DAVID: ...Mister Wray, gone away.

MEG: *(Startled)* Who?...When?

DAVID: Labor Day... So they say.

MEG: Are you trying to tell me something?

(DAVID *conjures up an old man in a wheelchair, as well as
his old dog.*)

DAVID: Old Billy Wray and his dog lived there—man
and dog—fourteen years—Billy Wray, so they say—
Terry the mutt—you can still smell him. *(He studies her
face.)* You don't have the flu, do you?

(MEG *turns away, her lips moving in silent prayer, she
makes the sign of the cross, stares out into the past. Below,
outside in a courtyard, the street-singer is heard again; his
voice, raw and Irish, bounces off the concrete canyon walls;
DAVID and MEG are pierced by the sound. Each is now
aware of the others' aloneness. The Angel of Death is passing
over. He sings in full voice.*)

STREET SINGER *(Off)*
...She died of a fever
And no one could save her
And that's how I lost my sweet Molly Malone.
Now her ghost wheels a barrow
Through streets wide and narrow
Calling cockles and mussels
Alive— Alive— O...
...God bless you, God bless you— Thank you very
much—good luck, God bless... Merry Christmas...

DAVID: ...Alive, alive— O... Throw him down some
change.

(MEG *is rapt*)

DAVID: ...Next time.

(MEG *stares out.*)

DAVID: Hey...wanta hear my John Barrymore take-off on Richard the "Turd"?

MEG: No thank you. Not now.

DAVID: "If not now, when?" As we say in Israel...
"Why, love forswore me in my mother's womb:
And, for I should not deal in her soft laws,
She did corrupt frail nature with some bribe
To shrink mine arm up like a wither'd shrub;
To make an envious mountain on my back,
Where sits deformity to mock my body;
To shape my legs of an unequal size;
To disproportion me in every part,
Like to a chaos, or an unlick'd bear-whelp,
That carries no impression like the dam!"

(MEG *turns back to look at the uncanny invocation of the great old actor.*)

MEG: Another time.

DAVID: When? Put your damn suitcase down. Tomorrow?

MEG: ...Tomorrow?

DAVID: "...Tomorrow, and tomorrow, and tomorrow,
Creeps in this petty pace from day to day,
To the last syllable of recorded time...
Life's but a walking shadow; a poor player,
That struts and frets his hour upon the stage,
And then is heard no more: it is a tale
Told by an idiot, full of sound and fury
Signifying nothing"

(MEG *finishes the last line with* DAVID. *Then, she makes her decision and crosses to 4B.*)

MEG: *(Turning back from the doorway)* "The Queen, my lord, is dead." *(She enters 4B.)*

DAVID: *(Daring to hope)* Yeah, well—Merry Krishnas.

(Inside 4B, MEG, at last, thumps down her heavy case. DAVID is saved!)

DAVID: And a satirical-rational new year!

MEG: *(Off)* Happy Chanukah!

(DAVID stiffens, then, with a cry of victory, both arms raised, he arches back in his wheelchair.)

DAVID: Warsawski!

(DAVID wheels into 4A, alive again! Singing the Woody Guthrie anthem along with Guthrie on the sound tape: "If you ain't got the do-re-me-...")

Scene 2
January, 1952, 1 A M—Eleven Months Later

(DAVID is sitting at the window, R., watching intensely, waiting for MEG to return. He spots her, adjusts his chair, pretends to be asleep.)

(MEG quietly and quickly climbs the stairs. She wears a threadbare but, originally, good ensemble, and carries a portfolio of theatrical material. She has removed her shoes, and is humming a Kurt Weil song, "Happy endings are the rule...")

(MEG has news and life to share with DAVID. She appears ten years younger than a month ago. She sees and hears him snoring. She studies him...smiles...tiptoes up...)

MEG: ...David...

(MEG strokes DAVID's hair. He pretends to jerk awake.)

DAVID: Where is he?!

MEG: Ssh...who?

DAVID: Godot.

(DAVID *and* MEG *begin suppressed giggles.*)

MEG: Shh.

DAVID: What do you mean? There's no one still alive in this *dump.*

MEG: Shh. Don't call this joint a dump.

DAVID: No, I mean where's your date, your escort, you know, your—

MEG: Oh, I see. Well—actually I was "alone on the aisle."

DAVID: Alone? Where was Warsawski sitting?

(DAVID *and* MEG *seethe with leashed laughter.*)

DAVID: Waiting for Warsawski! *(Shaking, silently) Waiting for Lefty!* ...No, seriously—did he come this time?

MEG: *(Silent hilarity)* ...Who?

DAVID: Godot!

(DAVID *and* MEG *finally recover.*)

DAVID: Was it great?

MEG: ...Great. The text. It was just a bootleg reading but you could—

DAVID: "I can't go on..."

MEG: "We will go on..."

DAVID: Jesus... You have to write about it tonight? Don't you want another drink?

MEG: Sure. I'll get it.

(MEG *disappears into 4A,* DAVID'*s apartment, singing to herself. He winces, then destroys the growing closeness between them with a lie.*)

DAVID: *(Calling)* I talked to him in Paris. Beckett. *Je n'en peu plus.*

MEG: *(Off)* Ssh. What? Are you serious? *(She emerges with drinks.)* Who cleaned up your place? You met *Beckett?*

*(*MEG *gives* DAVID *a chance and a choice to respect her by telling the truth. He stares out in anger.)*

DAVID: The V A sends someone over to clean up every two weeks... A man... Beckett? Hell, yes. *(Irish accent)* Sure, didn't we get pissed together? *(He glowers at her, lifts his glass.)* Cheers...

*(*MEG *defends herself with power enough to turn* DAVID's *face crimson with shame.)*

MEG: Was that during your "Irish" period when you got drunk with Bill Faulkner, and had your fistfight with Ernest Hemingway—or your Dylan Thomas binge, when the two of you burnt down a, what?, a livery stable—

DAVID: An *empty* livery stable.

MEG: ...Empty. It would be.

(She stalks away into her own apartment.)

DAVID: ...You secretly hate Jews, don't you?

MEG: You're drunk.

DAVID: No, I am not drunk. I am *a* drunk. And stay out of my g'damn apartment. *(British accent.)* "Kindly remember your place, Molly Malone: My residence, as you know, is, ah, 4A. While you, Miss Doolittle, squat in 4B". *(In his own voice)* 4A. "A" is "A," and "B" is "B" —never forget it— "A" is Number One, it comes First, and a long g'damn time later comes "B."

MEG: *(In her doorway)* And you're a dumb drunk and—

DAVID: And you hate men!

MEG: And you're a pathological liar, and you're an *alcoholic*, David—

DAVID: And you're a *Village View Virgin*, you're a Norman Mailer parasite and you have no sense of humor at all and you—

(MEG *rounds on* DAVID.)

MEG: You'll say anything! Shut up! It's Showtime! "Hey, Meg, did I tell you about how Studs Terkel told me I was a better writer than Nelson Algren!" Pathetic! And how you and Studs and poor old Nelson played poker together in a "table stakes" game every Saturday night on Division Street—oh, yes! —And how Nelson's lover, Simone de Beauvoir!, used to kibbitz, and she put her hand on your leg under the table. For God's sake! What a waste!

DAVID: Heil Hitler!

MEG: And how you and Studs were members of the Dill Pickle Club and orated to "The Great Throng" in Bughouse Square and Newbury Library! What a pathetic waste... What are you trying to prove? You're a decorated war hero, for God's sake!

(DAVID *and* MEG *pant in the silence.*)

DAVID: *(As Barrymore)* "Hath not a Jew eyes?"

MEG: ...So you think I hate *all* Jews? No. Only those who make the calculated choice to tell stupid lies that turn you into garbage so that no one in their right mind could possibly care for you. No—not all Jews. *(She goes back into 4B.)*

DAVID: Mm... Well, maybe with a couple of exceptions.

MEG: *(Off)* Oh?

DAVID: Yeah, Leopold Bloom...

(MEG *emerges with a drink.*)

MEG: He's a fictional character.

DAVID: Exactly...Jesus Christ, I guess, but, of course, he's a "fictional character", too, isn't he?

MEG: Ha-ha. You are dead wrong, boyo. Myself, I've known an army of Jewish intellectuals, and, believe me, it's made me a true believer in the sacred rite of circumcision.

DAVID: Watch out, now!

MEG: Why? *Circumcision*. It's perfect. You can always tell who's a real *prick*! *(Irish)* Jeers!

(MEG has traded blow for blow with DAVID, and he is beginning to know just who this woman is. As her door slams shut for the night, he raises a fist, as if to cheer her on to call his bluff.)

Scene 3
November, 1952, 10 P M—Eleven Months Later

Election night, 1952, eleven months later. MEG and DAVID sit glumly, each in their own doorway. From inside 4B, Meg's apartment, can be heard television coverage of the event, including the voices of candidates Eisenhower and Stevenson, respectively.

MEG: ...Come in. It's all over.

DAVID: No thanks.

MEG: Come in. You said it—Adlai Stevenson was Hamlet, and he never had a chance... Come in, I'll turn it off.

DAVID: You will? The T V? The ever staring Cyclopian eye?

MEG: It's over. He never had a chance. "But we must go on!"... Come in, I still have the stew from—

DAVID: *(Brogue)* Ah, the old Irish *stew*, is it?

MEG: *(Pause)*

It was good enough for you last night.

(MEG enters her apartment, closes door.)

DAVID: ...I'm sorry...Meg?... Come back.

(He wheels close to her door and sings a verse, in the old style, from "Danny Boy"... silence.)

DAVID: My father, and I am not joking, helped write speeches for Adlai Stevenson—don't talk to me about Stevenson—Adlai wasn't Hamlet... Can you hear me?

MEG: *(She comes to her door.)* The whole building can hear you... So he wasn't Hamlet.

DAVID: No. I was.

MEG: Oh. That's right. I forgot.

DAVID: That's because you never read the play.

MEG: "Goodnight, Sweet Prince... The rest is silence."

(MEG reenters her apartment and slams the door. DAVID searches for some cue that will bring her back... First, he tries the crippled Porgy's song from Porgy and Bess*:)*

DAVID: "Bess, you is my woman, now..."

(No response. Then, in desperation, the voice of Marlon Brando as Stanley Kowalski.)

DAVID: "...HEY, STELLAAAA!"

(A reaction from the building, as MEG opens her door and the Kowalski cry echoes.)

DAVID: ...I'm going on an eight-year drunk.

MEG: *Eight* years?

(MEG sits on the chair in front of her apartment.)

DAVID: That's right. To be followed by eight years of Richard Nixon. Make that a sixteen-year drunk...

What're you going to do, go back to Italy? (*Imitating her*) "Shh, Firenze," "The David," the, ah, by the way, "The David" was still circumcised—I mean at the time of your romantic wandering there with, what-was'-name, Ginsberg, Fred?, and you "were so happy, blah-blah-blah."

MEG: ...Jealousy is such a small trait. (*Pause. Then she sings a phrase from the losing Democratic Party's traditional song.*)
Happy days are here again
The skies above are blue again..."

(*Silence.* DAVID *drinks.*)

MEG: ...No. The last time I looked, someone had broken off your namesake David's young sex.

DAVID: ...Oh. And who would have done that? (*Brogue*) Pope Julius the Turd or you yourself?

MEG: Hmm... You think I want to castrate you, and every other man from "The David" on down. Oh, my, my. You may have read "every word of Freud" at the University of Chicago, but you don't have a clue, soldier.

DAVID: (*Pause*) Of course not. Why would you waste your time? I've been more or less "gelded" since 1945. And that was in Italy, too—but I lost my *bella figura* in Anzio, not in "Oh, so *molto, molto* Firenze."

(MEG *pales, jumping to her feet—*)

MEG: God dammit, David—forgive me.

(DAVID *stretches back in his chair, staring up at the skylight. His face is trapped in the winter spill of light from above.*)

(MEG's *compassion and character have pushed him over the edge of his lies, into the truth. He gestures her to keep her distance.*)

DAVID: ...What I'm actually going to do for the next eight years—is write the "Great American Novel" —about a spoiled brat from the North Shore of the Windy City of Chicago.

MEG: David—

DAVID: Whose father fixed him up with a desk job at Fort Sheridan so he could commute to the Wrigley Tower and write U S Armed Force Radio propaganda and—

MEG: I'm sorry.

DAVID: Who never heard a shot fired in anger because he was given leave every weekend to go to his family country club—good old Rolling Green *(Sings)* "Where the kikes and Ike Eisenhower play" —golf—so our hero could cheat at poker in the good old circumcised locker room, and lay all the wives of the boys who *were* over there in Anzio... And broke my spine, diving drunk into the pool one midnight, and left some poor bastard's equally insane and naked Gold Star wife and princess screaming for help... And was rescued from the wrath of his father's family and warehoused at the Veterans Hospital downstate... And got out with "life time disability" and wheeled my way here to this grand old Nazi neighborhood of Yorkville, and the kind clutches of the Warsawski ghetto—and the Manhattan V A who hauled him bodily up the four final flights, here, to good old 4A... *(At last he looks at* MEG, *ready to accept a death sentence—and his words are torn from him like pieces of flesh:)* And that's the "Great American Novel": fear-hate-cowardice-arrogance-cruelty-betrayal-and lies, lies, lies...

(Slowly, MEG *moves to* DAVID.*)*

MEG: ...Come in, for God's sake... *(She kneels at his side)* or will I do it for you here?

Scene 4
March 1954, 4 P M—Two Years Later

(Two years later. MEG is 34, DAVID 31. On the fourth floor both doors are closed. Sounds of someone ascending stairs. MARSHALL WARSAWSKI, the landlord, climbs into view, humming "Chicago".)

(WARSAWSKI is middle aged. He is fit and wears a deep suntan and a well cut top coat, scarf and hat. A college graduate who speaks with formal correctness, the landlord is a famous family man who harbors an immense secret life.)

(MEG is about to exit her apartment. When she hears WARSAWSKI, she hurriedly reenters. He reaches the landing and surveys this corner of his kingdom. He listens closely from the landing to the silence, then taps on the door of 4A.)

WARSAWSKI: Dave...Dave...Dave, it's Marshall.

(No answer. Silence. MEG cracks her door to peek out. WARSAWSKI and MEG stare at each other, until he tips his hat.)

WARSAWSKI: Miss McNally.

(Trapped, MEG emerges, carrying a suitcase.)

MEG: Mister Warsawski.

WARSAWSKI: Where's your "friend"? I didn't see him go out.

MEG: *(Locking her door)* Out? ...He doesn't go out. You know that. He can't go out. He has never gone out—except on Fridays—when they carry him to the Veterans Hospital.

WARSAWSKI: That is correct. And he never will... And how are you Miss McNally? What are you "studying" these days?

MEG: I teach. Part time. You know that, too.

WARSAWSKI: That is correct. "Part time." *(Knocking harder on 4A).* Dave. Dave—I have a letter from you father... Dave—a personal letter from your father— Judge Irving Light— Personal! *(Looks at* MEG's *suitcase)* Are you leaving us, Miss McNally?

MEG: *(Pause)* Ten days. I left you a note.

WARSAWSKI: Easter vacation? ...Back to Chicago? Good Friday at Saint Timothy's on West Van Buren? Isn't it funny how we're all from Chicago?

*(*DAVID *yanks his door open and wheels out at* WARSAWSKI, *bellowing the ditty "Chicago".)*

DAVID: "...I saw a man he danced with his wife in Chicago, Chicago—that's my home town!"

*(*WARSAWSKI *leaps away to save his Florsheims from* DAVID's *oncoming wheels.)*

WARSAWSKI: Whoa! Ha-ha! Watch the Florsheims. Whoa, whoa, whoa... How's the boy, Dave?

(A deadly silence. No one moves.)

DAVID: Do you know what time it is?

WARSAWSKI: Exactly 4 P M.

DAVID: By your "Elgin Executive"... It's the middle of the day. Are you trying to wake the dead?

WARSAWSKI: What? Oh, sorry, sorry. What are you writing now? —"Genius at work", Miss McNally, "Do not disturb." Ha-ha... No, I just *trotted* up to see if you needed any service, you know, because of Miss McNally's going back home for Easter Sunday, etcetera...

(All stare. WARSAWSKI *tips his hat again and starts down the stairs. Stops:)*

WARSAWSKI: Wait a minute. Your father. Judge Light. Special Delivery.

*(W*ARSAWSKI *turns back to hand* D*AVID* *the letter.* D*AVID* *does not take it.)*

DAVID: "Return to Sender."

(At length, W*ARSAWSKI* *turns, bows and sings to* M*EG* *and* D*AVID*, *then dances down the stairs still singing:)*

WARSAWSKI: "You'll have the time, the time of your life/I saw a man he danced with his wife/In Chicago... that toddlin' town, that toddlin' town..."

(Silence)

DAVID: ...Go ahead.

MEG: Here's the Lenny Bruce tape. Enjoy it...I'll be back on the—

DAVID: Fuck Lenny Bruce! I'm bigger than "Leonard Bruce". Laugh, you Catholic bitch, listen to this: "Ladies and Gentlemen, everybody knows that all communists are Jews, but did you know that all Jews are not communists? I kid you not. Some of them are socialists!"

MEG: That is terrible.

DAVID: Philistine.

MEG: But you can *write*.

DAVID: *(German accent)* So, you love me for my mind?

MEG: *(Pause)* That, too.

*(D*AVID* turns red and looks away.)*

DAVID: Go.

MEG: Will the V A send someone to—

DAVID: Disappear. "The House of Spirits— We Deliver."

MEG: *(Pause)* What?

DAVID: The House of Spirits.

MEG: Uh—you mean the—

DAVID: Right. The liquor store... "They deliver." The House of Spirits. You know: the father, and the son, and the holy smoke.

(MEG *contains herself and starts to leave with her suitcase.*)

DAVID: And don't forget to shack up with Warsawski at the Drake Hotel in Chicagoland! Ha-Ha!

MEG: *(From the stairs)* Write!

DAVID: Chicago, Chicago, that toddlin' town...
toddlin' town,
Chicago, Chicago,
I'll see you around...
See you around...

Scene 5
April 1954, 1 P M—Two Weeks Later

(*In the darkness, the voice of counsel JOSEPH WELSH as he eviscerates the demagogue, Senator Joseph McCarthy: "Have you, Senator, at long last, no shame...")*

(*Lights up on DAVID staring out the window, Right. He is in bad shape, trembling. A sound of someone coming up; he waits; MEG mounts into view.*)

DAVID: Who are *you*?

MEG: Did you get my four-page letter?

DAVID: Are you looking for a Miss Margaret Ann McNally? Well, it's a long story: she went back home to Chicago before Easter but she never came back. No, and it's a damn shame, too, but I'll tell you the whole tale because you see I'm a writer and I'm putting it all in my novel—

MEG: David—

DAVID: Well, you guessed it: she was really a simple Irish-American colleen who got in over her head, you know, writing material for Lenny Bruce, making up "Arts Reviews" for the *Village View* after they fired all the Communists— Anyway—she had a torrid affair with a notorious womanizer named M A Warsawski and, of course, she got knocked up and had to get an abortion somewhere—so Warsawski, who was not a Catholic, not at all, gave her a grand to go to Puerto Rico to have—

MEG: My mother had a stroke on Easter Sunday... She died on the Wednesday... The funeral was Saturday... the, ah...

(MEG bows her head, rooted to the top stair. DAVID covers his face, then wheels over and reaches out for her.)

DAVID: I never got your letter—*Warsawski!* So you know, I...I want you to lure Warsawski up here so I can cut his throat.

(MEG sits on her suitcase, next to DAVID's chair.)

MEG: Why are we living here on the fourth floor of a --

DAVID: I know, I know—you want a drink?

MEG: No... My head's splitting, the wake was a... Oh, God... I want you to write about her: five feet, built like a fullback, we called her the "Playmate of the Year"...

(MEG laughs and cries. DAVID strokes her.)

DAVID: I will. I'll write about Annie McNally and the Chicago Irish—I will— "We can't go on, we will go on." C'mon, sing her song?, how's it go, c'mon, I'm a veteran, that's an order!

(MEG has to laugh. DAVID starts her, and they sing the old Harry Lauder song, complete, finally, with music hall Scots accents, until she breaks.)

MEG: Just a wee deoch-an-Doris
Just a wee drop that's all
Just a wee deoch-an- Doris
Before we gang a-wa-..."

(DAVID *joins in,* MEG *sobs silently.)*

DAVID: That's it. C'mon, we'll sing her back to life!
And—

MEG: There's a wee wifie waitin'
in a wee but an ben
If you can say, "It's a braw bricht moonlight nicht
ye a'richt ye ken."
...Twenty-seven years in the Linen Room of Holy
Name Hospital—and him out of work—and his lungs
ruined—from the mines in Pennsylvania—

(All overlapping:)

DAVID: I'm going to write it all—I'm going to start
with—

MEG: Start with Glasgow—when they left Ireland—
before I was born. When they moved there and the
girls taught her to jump rope.
"Einie meine,
Macka racka
Rair rowe dominaka
Soominacke noominacki
Rum tum scum scoosh!"
Sing it with me.

DAVID & MEG:
"Einie meine,
Macka racka
Rair rowe dominaka
Soominacke noominacki
Rum tum scum scoosh!"

DAVID: Every word!

MEG: Up in the dark, winter and summer, four kids, him in his suspenders, coughing in the chair, sitting up all night trying not to cough so we could—

(All overlapping.)

DAVID: I got so drunk while you were gone, they had to send a team over from the V A—

MEG: She thought I should—she thought I lost my way here— She—

DAVID: She thought you should get—

MEG: "You're going' on thirty-five years old, Meg, and it's time, it's time—"

DAVID: I want you to marry me...I know what your mother would've—

(They both shake with laughter.)

MEG: Wait...wait... My brother's a policeman, he calls Joe McCarthy "Another Lincoln"!

(DAVID and MEG laugh and laugh.)

DAVID: I'll go on the wagon. No, I will, I'm going to write it, I'm going to tell the story of you and your family, and Chicago, and me and my family, and you can do the *typing* and save on *rent* and—

(One last upsurge of crying laughter, then silence.)

DAVID: ...This is not liquor talking...the V A wants to send a therapist over here. A psychotherapist. Because the—my, uh, sex, uh *impotenza*, as we say in—

MEG: Let's go inside.

DAVID: It could be *mental*...

MEG: ...What a character.

DAVID: You want to take off your g'damn girdle and try again.

MEG: David...

(DAVID wheels toward 4B.)

DAVID: C'mon, Lady Chatterly. Follow me into 4B. We'll put on your Edward R Murrow propaganda record and that'll make you so hot you'll have to tear it off— *(Imitation of Murrow)* —"Good night and good luck" —and then I—I will—I *will*—do something—for *you*...

(MEG crosses to sit on DAVID's lap.)

MEG: You already have.

DAVID: No, no, but I will, I will, I—

MEG: You've loved me. You've missed me, and you've pitied me, and—

DAVID: I never pitied you, I—

MEG: Shh— "Sure, there's nothing wrong with a bit of pity."

DAVID: That's your g'damn church talking now, no wonder Lenny Bruce fired you—

MEG: Shh -- and you've loved me...

(He sinks back, exhausted, as is she.)

DAVID: ...Meg...Meg...can we just—can we just...

(They rest, then sleep. In the dark, that voice of cultivated doom, Edward R. Murrow, quietly excoriates Senator McCarthy: "The Junior Senator from Wisconsin...")

Scene 6
July 1957, 11 A M—Three Years Later

(MEG is 37, DAVID 34, in 1957, three years later. The doors to 4A and 4B are closed. Footsteps coming up: THOMAS QUINN appears.)

(TOM is 40, a counselor with the Veterans Administration. A slight limp is the sign of his war wound in the South

Pacific. He is a recovering alcoholic [eight years], in charge of the Manhattan V A Alcoholics Anonymous program. He wears a hot weather shirt, speaks with a strong New England accent.)

(TOM reaches the landing. Silence, except for sounds below from the life of the building. TOM listens at 4A, then goes to 4B and taps lightly in code. Meg opens the door.)

MEG: Ah, Tom—I didn't want to bother you—on a Sunday.

TOM: It's better if I don't go near the church at all, these days.

MEG: Ah, Tom...

(They touch each other, almost shyly, then step apart. Music from below—Sinatra—up and then out.)

TOM: Geez, hotter than hell, eh? ...Is he alive or dead?

MEG: After he broke up the furniture—not a sound.

TOM: Your landlord called me on Friday.

MEG: Warsawski?

TOM: He wants him out. "Take him away to the V.A. Hospital" or he's going into court to get a "John Doe"/"Richard Roe" *eviction* order.

(MEG turns away.)

TOM: You can't, you're, ah—

MEG: I'm "part of the problem" now. Is that how you say it! "Co-dependent."

TOM: Yeah.

MEG: Even though I don't smoke or drink at all, anymore.

TOM: Even though he's still alive—thanks to you only.

MEG: Not anymore. I'm killing him now.

TOM: You're wrong.

MEG: I can't, I'm not—what he needs—I can't—a—love him the way he—

TOM: Listen to me: you're full of guilt because—

MEG: If I get out—

TOM: But you're wrong. He's killing himself.

MEG: If I could move—

(MEG *and* TOM *are both struggling to hold apart from each other.*)

TOM: And you're killing yourself. Only not with alcohol... You're in love with a married man—that's what's killing you... And that's what's killing me. Murdering me. You're not his "co-dependent," whatever the hell that means, you're mine.

(MEG *puts her arms around* TOM. *He holds back a return of her embrace, but the effort costs him.*)

MEG: He's—

TOM: He's just an innocent bystander...and he knows.

MEG: No, I've—

TOM: He knows. He's as quick as they come. He's a writer—he may never finish anything but he's a writer—and you can't fool him.

MEG: No.

TOM: He's a drunk—and a writer—and whatever guilt there is it's mine—

MEG: It's my fault—

TOM: Wait—it's mine, it's me—

MEG: Tom—

TOM: Wait—and it's me that's going to leave—

MEG: Tommy—

(A compulsive embrace, until MEG *and* TOM *have to step back.)*

TOM: I'm off his case, as of today—a man named Bob Buzzecki'll be in here tomorrow with a team— They'll break the door down, and take him out to de-tox.

(MEG *and* TOM *stand apart, eye to eye.)*

TOM: And I'll go to church with my wife and kids. *(She is shaking)* And then I'll go to confession, and take communion, and then...

MEG: *(A whisper)* What?

TOM: Nothing...I'll just remember you for the rest of my life... "One day at a time." —You know the words.

MEG: I know. "One day at a time."...And the other one: "Do the next right thing."

(MEG *and* TOM *are fighting for control.)*

TOM: That's it. That's A A. That's the chapter and the verse.

MEG: Goodbye, Tom... God bless.

(MEG *shakes his hand and retreats into her apartment.)*

TOM: *(Backing away)* "Here's looking at you, kid." "It's still the same old story..."

(TOM *cannot go on, he stumbles down the stairs.* MEG *comes running after him, trying to sing.)*

MEG: "...It's still the same old story/a fight for love and glory/a case of do or—David!"

(But TOM *is gone. And* MEG *swerves to 4A, hitting on the door with her head. Sick, holding her sides—she is secretly pregnant.)*

MEG: David—If you're alive—it's Sunday—David— It's Sunday and I'm going to make my "confession" to *you*: I'm not going anywhere—I'm staying here— As long as you stay, I stay. One day at a time...Tom's gone...and I'm here. Tom's off your case—because he cares so much. *(The silence from 4A forces her to make a wild effort.)* ...Oh, hello, Mister Bruce—oh, yes of course, I'll tell him you're here—David, listen, there's a Mister Bruce here to see you. *(As a ghastly Lenny Bruce:)* "Hello, 4A, how you doin', daddy? Listen, 4A, we need the room, man—we got a honeymoon couple here from Miami, Florida, who want to kill themselves, so we need the room."...

(MEG's last effort is spent. Her voice is failing, she slides down the door almost to the floor. Far below a baby cries and she, too, sobs silently, along with the child. Then, again, and exhausted, almost with numb self control: these words are forever.)

MEG: ...David... Wait for me. Tom's gone. We're here -- and we have to do the next right thing: That's it. That's all. "The next right thing, one day at a time." *(A whisper) David!*

(The baby's crying is hushed. Silence. Then, as the lights dim, the actual voice of Lenny Bruce covers the darkness :)

VOICE OF LENNY BRUCE: "...So, man—Jackie Kennedy—she was hauling ass over the back of the limo and the Secret Service... "

Scene 7
December 1964, 1 P M—Seven Years Later

(1964, MEG is 44; DAVID 41: seven years later. The two sit outside of their apartments with T V tables in front of them. On the trays are the remains of their lunch and writing materials. DAVID has grown a small beard and has a few gray hairs.)

(As they write, the sound of a Christmas carol drifts up. Then footsteps. Both pause, look, and wait.)

(T OM *appears. He is now 46, but looks older, his limp is worse. He is muffled up against the cold. The three look at each other, until* T OM *removes his old fur hat and* M EG *and* D AVID *recognize him.*)

(T OM *holds up a shopping bag containing presents. They stare, then* T OM *takes out three wrapped gifts and lays them on the landing.*)

(*Not a word yet spoken;* M EG *stands and* D AVID *wheels closer. Finally,* M EG *tries to start time again with an old refrain, murmured with her head on one side, like an ancient Irish woman.*)

M EG : ...Jesus, Mary, and Joseph.

(D AVID *reaches out slowly, to grip* T OM *'s hand.*)

T OM : That's us. (*Holding onto* D AVID *'s hand*) Meg, how did your *niece* used to say it?

M EG : "Matthew Mark *look* at John..."

(*And they all start to laugh, softly.*)

T OM : "Dominick, go frisk him."

(*Now the three are partly embraced and "laughing".*)

M EG : Take off your coat, Tom, and we'll give you a *soft* drink.

T OM : A soft drink. Is that all?

D AVID : Take off your coat, Tommy. Or as W C Fields said to the goat, that was in bed with him, that he thought was Mae West— "Take off your coat, my dear, or it won't do you the good when you go outside!"

(*They yelp with nervous laughter.*)

D AVID : 7-Up or Pepsi. Period.

T OM : "Sure, it's a good man's failin'" As my dear old drunk dad always said.

(*Laughter from all.* T OM *opens his coat.*)

TOM: 7-Up. Hold the bourbon.

(Still no one moves.)

TOM: "A good man's failing." What garbage... Now, they think it's genetic—for Ireland.

DAVID: Absolutely! And Chicago, too! What a crock.

(Laughter from all)

DAVID: 7-Up, coming up. *I'll* get it.

(DAVID wheels into 4A in order to leave MEG and TOM alone.)

(MEG pulls her old sweater tight around her.)

MEG: I'm getting fat...

(TOM breathes a half chuckle, and they continue their long lost gaze, moving slowly—but, DAVID wheels in with the soft drinks.)

DAVID: *(Wheeling) L'chaim.*

MEG: To Life.

TOM: "Here's looking at you," Uh...I like your beard... And your column in the *Village View*. As my old man would've said, "You've done very well in this country."

MEG: Mine, too.

DAVID: Thank you, Thomas.

MEG: Don't get him started on J F K and the—

TOM: You and Norman Mailer—you guys believe it was a conspiracy?

MEG: They do.

TOM: Yeah, well...me too...you guys starting up, uh—

MEG: They are.

DAVID: "Committee for the Truth about who killed J F K." Want to sign up, Thomas?

MEG: No.

TOM: Sure...

(Soft laughter, again. TOM *rebuttons his coat, looks at the presents.)*

TOM: Books... *(Puts on his gloves, then to* MEG*)* Teaching?

*(*MEG *nods slowly.* DAVID *sees her deep feelings and intervenes in a fake Irish brogue.)*

DAVID: Worrrld Literature. Chekhov, y'know, all them little fellas.

TOM: Chekhov. *(Shakes his head)* Nothin' ever happens.

(All laugh. TOM *turns on the landing as if to leave, putting on his hat.)*

TOM: Matt's waiting for me at Radio City.

MEG: *(Moving quickly)* Fourteen years old?

*(*TOM *pauses, with his back to them, ready to descend.)*

TOM: *(Nods)* ...My wife...Sheila—passed away in '61... So, now, I'm ...

MEG: Free?

TOM: Yeah.

(Silence. They are frozen in a parting tableau. At length, DAVID *releases them all.)*

DAVID: Mm... that makes three of us.

*(*TOM *turns back and he and* MEG *stare at* DAVID*.)*

(Recorded singing of Harry Lauder up and over into the interval.)

END OF ACT ONE

ACT TWO

Scene 1
September 1971, 11 A.M—Seven Years Later

(In the dark, sounds of war, riot, and protest music, including the voices of: Lyndon Johnson; Richard Nixon; Henry Kissinger; Tom Hayden; the young John Kerry; Malcolm X; Bobby Seale; Bob Dylan; late Beatles; all leading to the sounds of the Watergate crisis and the fall of the Nixon government: a sound capsule of 1963-1973.)

(In the dark, the sound of MEG *trying to master a song, and* DAVID *coaching her.)*

MEG: I'll get this. *(Sings Cat Stevens.)* Damn it!

DAVID: No, that's it, that's it.

(Lights up: DAVID *is teaching guitar to* MEG...Where Do the Children Play?*)*

MEG: I can't go on.

DAVID: But you vill go on... That's it. That's an order. *(More Cat Stevens.)*

MEG: I have to go to school. You are the world's worst, and the world's best teacher. Thank you. I love you.

*(*DAVID *and* MEG *kiss.)*

MEG: I have to go to school.

(MEG *starts to leave, pauses, looks at* DAVID, *then, returns, slips onto his lap: they kiss with prolonged passion.*)

MEG: *(Breathless)* I have to go to school.

(MEG *exits.* DAVID *arches in his chair holding his groin. He covers his frustration as he hears the voice of* JULIEN WARSAWSKI *greeting* MEG *on the stairs as he passes her.*)

(JULIEN, *the son of the late landlord, appears and trudges up to the landing. He is fifty—an overweight sad sack of stuttering contradictions and conflicts—a bundle of secrets and fears, but not unintelligent; in fact, deceptively cunning.*)

DAVID: Julien Warsawski.

JULIEN: *(Puffing)* H-hi.

DAVID: How you doing? How's your father, the lord of the land?

JULIEN: He p-passed away yesterday in Florida.

DAVID: Is that a fact?

JULIEN: Yeah.

DAVID: So... the old order passeth.

JULIEN: Yeah. I g-guess so.

DAVID: *(Pause)* So—was it sudden?

JULIEN: Yeah.

DAVID: In Miami?

JULIEN: Yeah. In a mo—in a mo—in a—

DAVID: A motel! Is that a fact? *(Pause)* Going to the funeral?

JULIEN: No, I'm a—I have a—I can't fly.

DAVID: Uh-huh... Me too. Well, we could have a little something here. You and me and Miss McNally. He was always, ah, fond of her.

JULIEN: W-well—

DAVID: With a few words from the old book "Ecclesiastes". What do you say?

JULIEN: W-well—

DAVID: "...for a living dog is better than a dead lion." ...That's you, isn't it, Julien? Me, too. Hm... My *pater* was a judge. Some said a corrupt judge. But a powerful judge. Now *your* father—he was, ah—

JULIEN: He w-was, he w-w-was—

DAVID: Precisely...so from one living dog to another: "May your tears be dried."

JULIEN: Thanks, Mister Light.

DAVID: ...I'll tell Miss McNally after her classes... Ah, about the rent...

JULIEN: Everybody else gets raised.

DAVID: Is that so? But not, ah—

JULIEN: No. Not you and M-miss M-McNally.

DAVID: Julien—Mister Warsawski—I thank you, sir.

(*Bowing,* JULIEN *turns to start down.* DAVID *stops him.*)

DAVID: Say, Julien—they had you enrolled in psychotherapy? Yeah, well, I know all about it. Be careful. Before you know it they'll be telling you that your old man was a phony and that you hated him—

JULIEN: W-w-well—

DAVID: And, that, in some way, you killed him.

JULIEN: W-W—

DAVID: It's a scandal. Men like us!... Why talk to strangers? You want someone to talk to—come up here. No charge!

(*They laugh.*)

DAVID: Uh, by the way—Julien—my cousin from Chicago's going to stay with me for a day or so, you know—till his ankle heals—he fell—off his bike, you know...

(Neither man moves. A siren starts far away. No movement. The siren comes closer. Lights to black.)

(In darkness: the siren screams in; gun shots and sirens overwhelm the audience's hearing. Then:)

(Sudden and total silence. A weak moonbeam through the skylight begins the next scene, with the voice of Elaine Brown crying out the Black Panther Anthem.)

Scene 2:
September 1971, 3 A M; sixteen hours later.

(Pale moonlight. MEG's door, 4B, is closed; DAVID's door, 4A, is cracked open only six inches—enough space for a lighted candle.)

(Someone can be heard climbing the stairs—a slow, soft scraping sound—and panting as he comes closer.)

(The MAN labors into sight and is forced to crawl up the final flight. DAVID's door opens another six inches.)

(The MAN reaches the landing, crawling now on all fours, a foot at a time. He is dressed in black. He is, in fact, a Black Panther fugitive.)

(The wounded black militant reaches DAVID's door. It swings open and the bleeding MAN falls over the threshold and is pulled inside by DAVID.)

(DAVID—after fifteen seconds—wheels out carrying a towel. He closes his door, moves to 4B and taps on MEG's door. Panther Anthem plays throug the entire scene.)

MEG: *(From inside)* ...David?

DAVID: Meg...

(A siren far away registers as MEG, *in her old bathrobe, unbolts her door and opens it. She is 51 years old in 1971.)*

MEG: *(Turning on a light)* David?

DAVID: Ssh. Turn it off!

MEG: *(Turning off the light and whispering)* What's wrong?

*(*DAVID *hands her a towel. The siren is closer now.)*

DAVID: Help me wipe up the blood.

(The siren is gone. DAVID *and* MEG *hold, then, blackout.)*

Scene 3
September 1971, 9 A M; One Week Later

(Apartment building and city sounds)

(Ron Hall, an F B I *Special Agent, glides silently up the steps: he checks the landing; listens at* DAVID's *door, 4A; looks out large window, R., and touches the brim of his hat in an obvious signal. He is 40, trim, with a Southwestern twang.)*

(From 4B, the F B I *hears* MEG's *voice singing and playing* Where Do the Children Play?. *He retreats to the stairs, out of sight, hand on gun. She comes out of her apartment and is locking her door, when he startles her:)*

F B I: *(Tipping his hat)* Margaret Ann McNally?

MEG: Hello?

F B I: *(Showing credentials)* Ron Hall, F B I.

MEG: *(Fighting to control her panic)* ...I see. *(Drops keys)*

F B I: Stand away from the door, please, ma'am. Thank you... Is Mister Light in this morning?

MEG: Mister Light? ...I'll check... He could be at the—ah, this is Friday—he could be out at the Veterans Hospital.

F B I: Right. That's right. He might could be... Could we talk just for a little bit?

MEG: Um, well, I have to be at work at, ah—

F B I: Ten o'clock. Hudson Academy. East Fourth Street... How you like it there? Better'n Pratt Institute?

MEG: *(Silence)* Can I help you—sir?

F B I: Ron. Ron Hall... Maybe. Yes, Ma'am, you might could. *(He looks around, at the landing.)* Top floor. No way but down from here, huh? *(Pause)* Meg—

(MEG reacts.)

F B I: You know a Negro male calls himself "Ahmeed Muhammed"?

MEG: What? No. No, I don't.

F B I: A K A "Big Man East."

MEG: No.

F B I: A K A Robert Holms.

MEG: No. I do not.

F B I: The "Minister for Information" —in the Black Panther Party, on the East coast.

MEG: No, sir.

F B I: Meg—I can help you. Can we go inside?

MEG: I'm going to work.

F B I: We can help you. *(Pause)* And you could help your country... Your brother—Detective Patrick McNally, Chicago P D— Now, I believe he would want you to protect yourself, wouldn't he? *(She puts her satchel down.)* Patrick, Pat— Can I talk to you like a brother, Meg? *(He moves close, lowers his voice.)* They're gonna mix you up in this thing any day now. I'm talking to you like a sister, Meg. They're gonna round 'em all up. All of you.

MEG: *(Backs up)* Who? Who is?

F B I: A T F—F B I—N Y P D— They've killed a police officer, now—and everybody's going down... Can we go on the inside?

*(*MEG *backs further away. The* F B I *agent crowds to her apartment door.)*

F B I: Can we go in and call Chicago? *(No response)* Talk to your brother Pat. He'll tell you what's right. Pat'll tell you, how Mister Light and these cop killers're gonna set you up.

(The F B I agent moves in. MEG *labors to control her breathing.)*

F B I: Sell you out. Set you up. Will you give me your key? ...Pat'll tell you: It's a crazy time: A single woman. White men. Black men, Jews, all mixed up. A single white woman all mixed up. A crazy time, Margaret... This is a criminal conspiracy, Meg. Your choice: Go down with the terrorists—or come home—to your Saviour—and to America.

(The moment holds as the hot September light fades to black.)

Scene 4
September 1971, 11 P M; Thirteen hours later.

(The moon through the skylight. DAVID *and* MEG *sit side by side on the landing, conversing, throughout, in covered tones in the darkness.)*

DAVID: ...Start over. You went to class?

MEG: ...I suppose so.

DAVID: What do you mean?

MEG: I don't know. I'm in a state of shock.

DAVID: You didn't go back in—he left first?

MEG: David—

DAVID: Bugs!

MEG: What've you done?!

(DAVID *makes a slow, wide gesture.*)

DAVID: "Bugs."

MEG: What?

DAVID: Wiretaps.

MEG: ...What are you doing? David?

DAVID: *(Gesturing)* General terms. No names.

MEG: David, you—

DAVID: Talk in *general—terms.*

(DAVID *puts his hand over* MEG's *mouth. They stay thus until she slowly frees herself. Their voices remain leashed in.*)

MEG: David—you put blood on my hands!

(DAVID *puts his hand over* MEG's *mouth again, but this time with force, and uses his other hand to grip her head.*)

(DAVID *leans in to pour a story into her ear.*)

DAVID: Listen: there was a war, there-is-a-war. And we lost—

MEG: Ahh—David—

DAVID: Just listen. *(He lets her breathe.)* They're tapping our phones. No question, and who knows what else, plus Warsawski, that— Shh! *(He wheels to stairs, listens intently... At length:)* That loveable bundle of secrets, Julien Warsawski, has to be their main informer in this building. So from now on—we are not alone. Never. Ever. So conduct your conversation accordingly. No problem. Because everybody who has ears or can read,

already knows that I'm an anarchist, and that you're
a non-violent failed Catholic virgin saint and I R A
apologist.

(But MEG *does not smile in the dark at this murmurous
but sharply articulated attempt at re-establishing personal
contact.)*

MEG: They killed a policeman.

DAVID: You mean the "Just Assassins" of 1907—in the
Russian—

MEG: And they would kill my brother.

DAVID: And my father, if he were still alive. Referring
to the Ku Klux Klan of—

MEG: Your father, my brother, and—

DAVID: The late Judge Light. I am, I was his informer.
The late Light and your All-American fullback brother
don't mean a thing in this war we're talking about—in
"general terms".

*(*MEG *sits down again, with* DAVID, *in darkness.)*

MEG: Where do you go every Friday?

DAVID: The V A. Where do you think?

MEG: No, you don't...I don't know you.

DAVID: You don't? Who do you think comes in here
and carries this goddamn infernal machine down four
flights every—

MEG: I don't know. I don't believe anything, now.

DAVID: Good! The sweet little Catholic girl in the white
shoes grows up and teaches her first grade students to
go home and cut their mommy's and daddy's throats.
Right on!

MEG: You are insane. I'm not talking about your
old time drunks and rants. But right now: cool and

calculating—and crazy. I know you but I don't know
you.

(DAVID *wheels in, close to* MEG's *face.*)

DAVID: But I know you, Margaret Ann McNally. I
know you deeper than you know yourself. I know that
you're planning to run away—tomorrow—from all this
"insanity" —these bad niggers and good G-Men—shut
up! (*He covers her mouth, by force again.*) You're gone—
off to sunny Italy. To Firenze—to find Fred. Huh?
Good old Fred with his magic Jewish cock—when you
were young and poor, when you sold the bottles you
and Fred collected for a few *lire*—for a down payment
on all your hopes and dreams—when you were young
and "Chicago was ready for reform." Hallelujah!

(DAVID *releases* MEG *as she crumples in silence. His head
hangs, too, now.*)

(MEG *begins to recover. As she does, her breathing changes
until, suddenly, she hurls herself on* DAVID, *beating him.*)

MEG: ...Who are you! —Who are you!

(MEG *wears herself out.* DAVID *does not defend himself.
Silence and immobility. A distant street sound*)

DAVID: ...You want to go to Italy—together? —adopt a
black kid? I don't give a damn. This country's extinct.
Walt Whitman predicted it— "The most tremendous
failure of time." We read that together. Didn't
we? In the good old days when I was an apolitical
dipsomaniac and you were a Chicago Democratic
do-gooder out to save my soul. Well—you saved it,
"Major Barbara!" (*Sings the old Salvation Army parody*):
"Hallelujah, Hallelujah/Put a nickel on the drum/
Save another drunken bum/Hallelujah..." (*Broken*)
Hallelujah... Yeah. And who was it that showed me
the "self portraits" that your first grade black kids
drew for you--when you were at Roosevelt taking your

Masters'?...I may be nothing but a dry drunk and a
liar posing as an author *manqué*, but you're the famous
Meg McNally, Princess of the working class, and it
was you, or was it not? who showed me those –those
unspeakably—ah, Jesus Christ—those unspeakably
obscene self-drawings of those black children?

(MEG *gathers all her strength, then stands up to the truth.*)

MEG: It was.

DAVID: The little stick figures?

MEG: Yes.

DAVID: With a head and legs?

MEG: Yes!

DAVID: But no arms? —It made me sick! —Where were
their arms? ...If you're a human being—tell me what
you told me then.

MEG: (*Bracing*) They had no arms.

DAVID: No. No arms. Only stumps, little, ah, flippers,
instead of arms—why?

MEG: (*Full force*) Powerless.

DAVID: They were "powerless" —you said—so that's
why, when they drew their own body images, they did
not draw *arms*, like white kids did—and you published
the actual drawings in your thesis and you won a prize
and you told me—damn you! —if they don't find the
strength, somewhere, to love and work—the *arms*—
then, someday, they will pick up other "arms"— *"other
arms"* —and that will be the end... And I had no legs,
and they had no arms—

(MEG *reaches out for* DAVID.)

DAVID: And I believed you. And it came true.

(*They breathe.*)

DAVID: True...

(DAVID *and* MEG *lie in each other's arms until they sleep. A siren, far off, recedes.*)

Scene 5
January 1981, 11 A M: Ten Years Later

(*The sound rising under the scene's opening is that of Ronald Reagan's voice as he recites his inaugural address to the nation: "...the city on the hill...")*

(MEG *and* DAVID *are in their respective apartments. The new President's echoing words reach them from all the television sets in the building, and the world, except their own.* MEG *is, now, 61;* DAVID *58.* DAVID'*s new wheelchair is motorized.*)

MEG: *(Off)* Are you going to be able to stand it? *(In her doorway)* ...David?

DAVID: *(Off)* What?

MEG: *(Sings)* "Arise ye prisoners of starvation."

DAVID: *(Enters)* The purple hair.

MEG: We can't go on.

DAVID: The ice cream suit.

MEG: But we must go on. Can you stand it? ... I mean... can you?

(DAVID *and* MEG *look long at each other, recalling, vividly, crisis situations from their past: love, sex, alcohol, politics, near suicide.*)

DAVID: ... ight years of that?

(MEG *smiles grimly.*)

DAVID: "The City on the Hill," the "New Jerusalem"?

(MEG *kisses* DAVID's *hand.*)

DAVID: No. Not really...can you?

MEG: What's the "cherce"?

(DAVID *stares away, again, into space.*)

MEG: Finish your novel...

(DAVID *and* MEG *begin to laugh.*)

MEG: I retire in June. I'll type the final draft.

(*Laughing,* DAVID *sings a refrain from* The Threepenny Opera. MEG *joins him.*)

DAVID: "Light 'em up, boys
Light 'em up, boys
Happy endings are the rule."

(DAVID *and* MEG *sit and stare, then she rises and begins a series of intense dance exercises.*)

MEG: ...You better join me.

(DAVID *laughs bitterly.*)

MEG: C'mon, put 'em up. C'mon, Golden Boy!

DAVID: Ha, ha—come on, Lorna Moon.

(MEG *dances around* DAVID*'s chair, shadowboxing, until he begins to punch hard at her open palms.*)

MEG: That's it—you're a contender—King Levinski! The "Hebrew Hope"!

(DAVID *gives a roar of laughter and they both stop to recover and breathe.*)

MEG: ...So— "to be or not...", etc.

(DAVID *begins to glow with an idea;* MEG *catches the fire.*)

DAVID: ...You know who Hamlet's father was?

MEG: What? I knew his mother.

DAVID: "Leave her to heaven." No, who was his father? I'll give you a clue: it wasn't the ghost with the clanking balls, and it wasn't his twin brother Uncle Claudius...

MEG: Ha! Who? Ronald Reagan?

DAVID: Close, you're close. But Reagan's a sad, mad clown—Hamlet's old man was a wise fool.

MEG: ...You mean—

DAVID: *Yorick!* The king's jester— "Here hung those lips that I have kissed I know not how oft... He hath carried me on his back a thousand times..." Get it? The "antic disposition", the soldiers, the actors, the pirates, the grave diggers—these're Hamlet's people—*this is "The Yorick Axis"*!

*(*DAVID *is transported, tries to stand!* MEG *embraces him.)*

MEG: *The Yorick Axis*: that's a book, that's an elegant meditation, that's—

DAVID: *(Loud)* Forget it!... "The rest is silence."

MEG: You forget it, Levinski—you're not Prince Hamlet, not yet, you're—

DAVID: I'm—*who*?

*(*DAVID *and* MEG *stare at each other.)*

MEG: You're the Shakespeare of East 87th Street, and "this too, shall pass"!

DAVID: Oh, no, this one "shall not pass." Not this clown. He's going to make them wish they had Richard Nixon back again.

MEG: Ha! That's good. Put it in the book.

DAVID: And you'll type it all up?

MEG: I *will*.

DAVID: Like the Countess Tolstoy?

MEG: Exactly.

*(*DAVID *and* MEG *cannot help laughing.)*

MEG: Seriously...

DAVID: It's unreadable, I can't finish it.

MEG: Why not?

DAVID: I don't know... Because I'm not Tolstoy...

MEG: No, you're Dostoevsky.

DAVID: Ah-hah, *I don't know*!

MEG: *(Pause)* All right—how about Plan B?

DAVID: Suicide?

MEG: That's Plan C. Plan B is your old friend, and mine: "One day at a time."

DAVID: Ahh— "One Day at a Time." Does that include, *(Irish)* "Do the Next Right Thing?"

MEG: Amen.

DAVID: And what would that be?

MEG: The next right thing? For you? You tell me.

DAVID: ...For you, then.

MEG: Me? Well-for a start...Don't go to Italy.

(DAVID and MEG have to laugh again.)

DAVID: You still think about it?

MEG: Italy?

DAVID: Sex.

MEG: Sex?

DAVID: Sex, Italy: same thing. *El mismo.*

MEG: That's Spanish... Sex? I'm sixty-one years old.

DAVID: Oh, for Christ's sake. *(Irish)* "You're no age at all."

MEG: As my mother would've said.

DAVID: ...Do you? ...Tom Quinn?

MEG: ...Tom?

DAVID: I used to, ah, picture the two of you.

MEG: ...I know.

DAVID: I know you did... Did you mind?

MEG: No.

DAVID: ...You know—if the *Pater* hadn't—if my g'damn father'd left me anything, I'd give it all—

MEG: Don't insult me, David.

DAVID: Every dirty dime. Because I—

MEG: Let's have a cup of—

DAVID: Because I don't intend to linger.

MEG: "Linger"? We're supposed to be talking about *today*.

DAVID: Ahh, oh, "Today!"

(DAVID *and* MEG *laugh.*)

MEG: January 20, 1981.

DAVID: "Inauguration Day!" The day the shit-storm started.

MEG: Now you're awake. Preach!

DAVID: Day One of the shit-storm— You don't want to talk about you and Fred in Florence thirty-five years ago?

MEG: No.

DAVID: No, you don't want to hear my dream about that, then?

MEG: I don't care what you dream about. I'm interested in what you *write* about.

DAVID: What if it's the same thing?

MEG: All right—then write about it. If your dream is the next "right" thing, then *write* about it. I give you permission. *(She takes his hand.)* I give you my body and my soul. Take it! Take me—and tell my story: the whole Irish/American/Italian/ African/Jewish *dream of* it!

(DAVID *studies* MEG *with huge eyes, like a child.*)

DAVID: You—give me— "permission"?

MEG: ...I give you everything... *Tutto, ogni cosa.*

(DAVID *and* MEG'S *intimacy is complete: lovers, mother-child, friends, comrades.*)

(*The building and street sounds sink towards silence.*)

DAVID: Well...all right...go in and get my notebook, then—and a *pencil*...

(DAVID *will live.* MEG *has prevailed. Their laughter is deep and long.*)

(*In the darkness, Woody Guthrie sings "This Land is Your Land".*)

Scene 6
January 2005, Noon: Twenty-Five Years Later

(*The door to 4A stands open. Paraphernalia for painting* DAVID'S *former apartment, including a small ladder, crowds the entranceway. It is twenty-five years since the last scene. The wheelchair is parked near his door.*)

(MEG, *aged 85, and* TOM, *89, climb the last flight of stairs, pausing twice to catch their breath. Both use canes. A heroic effort brings them up to the landing.*)

(MEG *and* TOM *do not remove their overcoats, because of the cold.*)

(*Adlibs, about Chicago and funeral.*)

TOM: Who was that they made a fuss about?

MEG: Roger Ebert.

TOM: The fat one. The skinny one went first. That was a shocker.

MEG: I'll put the kettle on. Do you want to use the bathroom?

TOM: No. I'll help you.

(Below in the courtyard, an Irish street singer. MEG sits. TOM looks for change for the singer, but she has not yet unlocked her door.)

TOM: ...You certain that was Norman Mailer standing behind that, uh, big—

MEG: That was him.

TOM: Well, why didn't he say anything to you?

MEG: Who knows? Maybe he had nothing to say.

TOM: Mailer?

(MEG and TOM chuckle.)

MEG: I'll put the kettle on.

TOM: I'll help you.

MEG: Rest your leg.

TOM: It's not so good today.

(TOM crosses and sits on the step ladder, at 4A.)

MEG: Would've been worse if you had to kneel.

(MEG and TOM laugh.)

TOM: No church for me. Doctor's orders.

(MEG and TOM laugh.)

TOM: But it went off just right. You arranged it just right.

MEG: How he would've hated it all.

TOM: Not the Woody Guthrie tape.

MEG: No.

TOM: *(Sings)* "This land is your land..."

MEG: *(With volume)* "This land is my lands, from California to the New York island."

TOM: He loved you.

MEG: ...Ahh—the tea?

TOM: I won't say no. Well, you saved his life. And he knew it.

MEG: *(Pause)* He made me laugh.

TOM: *(Pause)* Is that why you stayed on here... The key.

MEG: And he had courage.

TOM: Courage? ...It's true.

MEG: ...Made me laugh.

(MEG gives TOM the key, at last.)

TOM: You laughed like hell when he—that time when he said Clinton—during the sex thing—he said, um, a, Bill Clinton was Tom Sawyer *pretending* to be Huck Finn, and you—what the heck was that supposed to—

(MEG laughs again, hard. So does TOM.)

MEG: And then he quoted Lear, didn't he?

TOM: Who?

MEG: *(Laughing)* King Lear— "Adultery? Thou shalt not die for adultery..." He could make you laugh.

TOM: Hmm... What about me? I made you cry. Ha-ha.

MEG: ...You're the one who saved his life.

TOM: Not me. A A...

MEG: "One day at a time."

TOM: One *hour*—now.

(Showing his watch. MEG and TOM laugh.)

MEG: Literally.

TOM: *(Pause)* So, I'm the one who made you cry.

MEG: ...You're the one who made me walk the floor all night.

TOM: It was killing me, too. The guilt. *(He enters 4B to make the tea.)*

MEG: The "guilt." The guilt is highly overrated. With me and guilt, it was—I was like a dog with a bone... *(Chuckles)* Their wives never understood me.

TOM: What's that? Who?

MEG: You didn't think, did you Tommy, that you were the only married man?

TOM: *(In the doorway)* ...Oh.

MEG: Except for David, and, ah...

TOM: *(Pause)* I used to, uh—

MEG: And Italy, a long time ago... That was my first child.

(TOM starts to cross back toward 4A. This stops him.)

TOM: ...What's that? You had a—

MEG: The first child—I never had.

TOM: Wait a minute.

(TOM is staggered, but makes the cross to sit on the ladder again. MEG wheels DAVID's chair next to him and sits.)

MEG: ...Then there was yours?

TOM: Mine?

MEG: Ours. The one we never had. The one I never told you. The one I left in Puerto Rico.

(No sentiment. All courage. TOM grips MEG's hand.)

TOM: Jesus... But not with—never with Dave—

MEG: Tom—jealousy's such a small trait... No, David aborted his *novel*, that's all.

TOM: Why?

MEG: *(Laughs)* He claimed he couldn't finish it until he decided whether to spell America with a "C," or a "K" ...No, the babies were mine. And two more later. Quite a brood, hmm?

TOM: Jesus... Oh, Jesus...

MEG: Never mind, Tommy, never mind...I had them—for a while—I carried them. They were *mine*—

(TOM rises.)

MEG: Sit down now please, Tommy, before you fall down.

(Slowly, TOM recovers, looking into the dark 4A. His shoulders shake.)

TOM: Who's moving in here now?

(MEG and TOM laughing together)

MEG: I don't know, but if he's a drinker, you'll be the one I call.

TOM: *(Pause)* Well, I'll be dropping by. *(Returns her keys.)*

MEG: You better.

(TOM crosses around MEG to the stairs.)

TOM: Meg...I, ah... We, ah, could...

(MEG is looking out. She is somewhere else. Her lips are moving. Is she praying? Then she laughs softly and murmurs:)

MEG: Ed Solomon...

(TOM turns and realizes that MEG is, literally, recalling DAVID, talking to him. And to her mother.)

MEG: ...Tolstoy...Matthew Mark look at John... *(Singing softly)* "...Just a wee drop that's all..."

TOM: *(A murmur)* Goodbye, Meg...God bless...

(TOM *limps slowly, laboring to make no noise. He starts down the stairs while* MEG *is still communing with a lost world.*)

(MEG *is alone. Her voice is very soft and vibrant.*)

MEG: *Basta, basta, troppo. (A young woman's laugh) La Commedia, ha, ancora, ancora!*
Just a wee deoch-an-doris
Just a wee drop that's all
Just a wee deoch-an-Doris
afore we gang a-wa."

(*Laughing softly with the joy of life of a young woman, unaware of the tears or the years, as she drops off to sleep in the wheelchair.*)

Scene 7
September 2006, 9 P M:
A Year and Eight Months Later

(MEG, *86, sits in* DAVID's *wheelchair in the half dark of the Indian summer evening, dozing, as she listens to a Chopin medley playing at a low volume in her apartment.*)

(*Sounds below, on the stairs, become a young man dragging a suitcase up to the fourth landing. This will be* VICTOR GORDON, *early 20's. [To be portrayed by the actor playing the Black Panther]*).

(VICTOR *does not see* MEG *sitting in the gloom until he almost stumbles over her.*)

VICTOR: Hah! Jesus!

(MEG *half catches him, and holds on.*)

MEG: Careful. Watch your step.

VICTOR: ...Mrs Mac-A-Nally?

MEG: *Ms* McNally. Who else?

(MEG and VICTOR laugh a little.)

VICTOR: I've heard all—I've heard all about you.

MEG: Mm.

VICTOR: *(Shaking hands)* I'm Victor Gordon.

MEG: ...What's "Gordon"?

VICTOR: Gordon?

MEG: Scottish?

VICTOR: I really don't know. It's made up. I'm from San Juan.

MEG: Puerto Rico? ...Tourist? Terrorist? *Terrorista?* —Ha-ha.

(Slowly, MEG and VICTOR begin to smile, and relax.)

MEG: Puerto Rico. A-ha—you would be *por se questo?* ...You must be an actor, then.

(MEG and VICTOR laugh a little.)

VICTOR: Well—a dancer.

MEG: *Bailarin?*

VICTOR: *Si. Bailarin. (He moves to look at 4B.)*

MEG: Come back, ah, come a little closer... Mm: a Scottish dancer from Puerto Rico... It could be.

(More friendly laughter.)

VICTOR: A Scottish dance *student* from—

MEG: I'll make us some ice tea—or, ah, we'll send out for, ah, ah, you know the, ah, ice cone with—

VICTOR: *Paraguas!*

MEG: *Paraguas!* Strawberry! Ha! ...Then, you can tell me all about it. *Dime todo.*

(MEG and VICTOR are both salivating and laughing.)

MEG: Ah, but, first— *Primero*... I'd like to see you dance.

VICTOR: *(Pause)* Now?

MEG: Why not? No?

VICTOR: ...I don't—

MEG: Use the landing. The banister. The stairs. No one comes up here anymore. Use my music, use the Chopin —"Impromptu" ... *Use, use...*

(MEG *and* VICTOR *look at each other in the fading, late summer light. Silence as the Chopin plays. Her power grips him.)*

(Then, VICTOR *pushes his baggage aside and removes his shoes and socks.* MEG *enters 4B, to turn up the volume of the music.)*

MEG: That's right... And your shirt... Everything. *Todo.*

(Volume up. VICTOR *panics, picking up his shoes and socks, and reaching for his suitcase—but* MEG *reenters, and stands in her doorway. She turns off the light on the landing next to her door.)*

*(*VICTOR *is caught at the head of the stairs. He removes his shirt.* MEG *gasps at the beauty of his youth, leans back, breathless against her door frame, then pushes herself into motion.)*

MEG: *Todo!*

*(*MEG *crosses, circles the entire stage, head turned front, as if to give* VICTOR *privacy to disrobe completely.)*

MEG: I'm an 86-year-old woman, Victor—but I'm still a woman.

*(*MEG *has reached the dark opening of 4A; enters, communes with* DAVID's *ghost. Turns off his landing light. Then stares at* VICTOR.)*

VICTOR: God they were not lying about you downstairs.

(Then, in the descending darkness, at last, VICTOR takes off his jeans, leaving only his ragged boxer shorts, and stands there on the stairs, looking up at MEG.)

(MEG crosses the front of the stage as if putting VICTOR's name up in lights on Broadway.)

MEG: ... That's right... Now, dance for me... "The Dance of the New Tenant"...And then we'll decide on what your name should be: Gordon, or Gonzales, or Ginsberg, whatever...

(Finally, VICTOR backs down the stairs, out of sight for a moment.)

(MEG watches the empty steps until, suddenly, VICTOR springs into sight and begins "The Dance of the New Tenant.")

(VICTOR's improvisation carries him, eventually, up the steps to the landing. There, he dances out the identity struggle of his new generation.)

(MEG urges VICTOR on, as he tires and tries to stop. He is confused. She directs him, pointing to the dark 4A.)

MEG: *Mas! Mas! Arriba. 4A! 4A!*

VICTOR: 4A?

MEG: *Si, Si...4A!*

(VICTOR starts to dance into 4A; pretends to meet a monster. Fights with the devil, boxes, scores a knockout, laughs! But is, actually, afraid to enter.)

VICTOR: *(Declaring victory)* La Lucha!

MEG: *La Lucha Continua! Compañero!*

(VICTOR collapses into the wheelchair.)

VICTOR: 4A, no.

MEG: *Mas, muchacho. 4A! Hijo! Levantate! 4A! Yes! 4A,
coraje! Courage!*

VICTOR: No!

(VICTOR *backs away from 4A toward 4B.* MEG *holds onto
him: "No"; "Si"; "No"; "Si". Then she, too, calls out "No,"
in unison with the youth. Holding him, they give birth
together: "No—noooh—nooooh—)*

MEG & VICTOR: No, no, no, no... *Nosotros!*

(VICTOR *gathers his powers: and at the apogee of the music
cries out Nosotros! And flashes through the air—out of the
last light and into the blackness of the waiting 4A.)*

(MEG, *where she stands, arches in ecstasy!)*

MEG: ANCORA!

END OF PLAY

www.ingramcontent.com/pod-product-compliance
Lightning Source LLC
Chambersburg PA
CBHW052223090426

42741CB00010B/2658